SUMMARY:

Emotional Intelligence

Why it can matter more than IQ

ABBEY BEATHAN

Text Copyright © Abbey Beathan

Legal & Disclaimer

The information contained in this book is not designed to replace or take the place of any form of medicine or professional medical advice. The information in this book has been provided for educational and entertainment purposes only.

The information contained in this book has been compiled from sources deemed reliable, and it is accurate to the best of the Author's knowledge; however, the Author cannot guarantee its accuracy and validity and cannot be held liable for any errors or omissions. Changes are periodically made to this book. You must consult your doctor or get professional medical advice before using any of the suggested remedies, techniques, or information in this book. Images used in this book are not the same as of that of the actual book. This is a totally separate and different entity from that of the original book titled: "Emotional Intelligence"

Upon using the information contained in this book, you agree to hold harmless the Author from and against any damages, costs, and expenses, including any legal fees potentially resulting from the application of any of the information provided by this guide. This disclaimer applies to any damages or injury caused by the use and application, whether directly or indirectly, of any advice or information presented, whether for breach of contract, tort, negligence, personal injury, criminal intent, or under any other cause of action.

You agree to accept all risks of using the information presented inside this book. You need to consult a professional medical practitioner in order to ensure you are both able and healthy enough to participate in this program.

Table of Contents

The Book at a Glance

Chapter 1 talks about how certain emotions propel people to safety or danger, tragedy, or success. It also discusses the primitive brain and its evolution over time. Emotional responses also have underlying reasons and direct people's actions.

Chapter 2 talks about the amygdala and the hippocampus that are responsible for emotions. It also talks about how emotional outburst or feelings can either bring positive or negative results. Emotional reactions can also be destructive or beneficial.

Chapter 3 talks about the differences between emotional intelligence and mental intelligence. Emotional intelligence is important when it comes to establishing solid relationships, maintaining cooperation, and making crucial decisions in life.

Chapter 4 discusses self- awareness and how being aware of one's emotions is beneficial in making decisions. You will also read about situations of people who have lost emotional awareness due to prefrontal surgery.

In chapter 5, you will learn about negative feelings such as anger, sadness, and dealing with these feelings. You will also learn about different levels of anger and sadness.

In chapter 6, you will learn about how moods and anxiety affect performance. You will also encounter the "flow model" which is the peak of emotional intelligence.

Empathy is evident even in infancy, as chapter 7 points out. A child's upbringing affects his emotional intelligence, as proven by the level of empathy he or she has. Morality is also rooted in empathy. This chapter also explains criminals' behavior in relation with apathy, which is the opposite of empathy.

In chapter 8, you will learn about how emotions play a part in building or destroying relationships. How one controls the emotions also determines social competence.

Marriage is the best example of how gender differences are factors in emotional intelligence. Men and women have different methods of handling and responding to emotions, which result in marital conflict, as discussed in chapter 9. Much of these emotional responses are rooted in childhood, parenting, and social norms.

In chapter 10, you will learn about the importance of emotional intelligence in the workplace. Emotional competence means there are no dominant bosses, and employees work harmoniously and respect diversity. Prejudices will also be absent if employees are emotionally intelligent. You will also learn about the importance of collective emotional intelligence in companies.

Emotional intelligence in the form of compassion and empathy is crucial in medical care. In chapter 11, patients recover quicker when doctors and nurses are compassionate. Anxiety, depression, and negative emotions make people more prone to diseases and infections.

In chapter 12, you will learn how the family is crucial to a child's emotional intelligence. How a child is treated as early as infancy determines how he or she behaves later in life.

Chapter 13 talks about post-traumatic stress disorder and that one's emotions can be relearned through psychotherapy. Adults and children have different ways of dealing with stressful or traumatic events.

Chapter 14 talks about in-born temperaments that are due to an over-excited amygdala. These temperaments can still be changed depending on parental upbringing and environment. One crucial point is awareness and understanding emotions.

Chapter 15 talks about childhood and adolescent

misbehaviors that stem from being emotionally incompetent. The factors are biological make-up, relationship with parents, parental upbringing, and the social environment.

In chapter 16, you will learn that emotional literacy is still possible through intervention programs especially in schools. The goal is to teach children to become self-aware, be emphatic, and handle their emotions appropriately.

Aristotle's Challenge

The memory of a middle-aged, black driver who affected everyone with his positivity offered a realization that psychology is a powerful tool. As he greeted passengers and shared his insights on the passing scene, he was able to share his enthusiasm that by the time everyone got off the bus, they were feeling better than they did.

Aristotle tells us that anger is easy to exhibit. The challenge is how to be angry with the right person, at the appropriate time, degree, method, and purpose. The positive incident above provided an irony to the negative events announced in the newspaper. There were incidents of students who became violent due to bullying and name-calling. There were even accounts of murder due to parental abuse.

It is important to determine how to make sense of certain negative emotions and how to address them.

Why This Emotion Now

Numerous scientific studies aim to study the brain and emotions. Scientists use the neurobiological data to understand how the brain works and which parts of the brain are responsible for emotions.

The studies bring to light the argument between the importance of IQ versus emotional intelligence. Studies show that emotional intelligence can be taught and that individuals can be trained to control the emotions. Two important morals develop from emotional intelligence: compassion and self-restraint.

Part One:

The Emotional Brain

Chapter 1: What Are Emotions For?

One significant example that shows the power of emotions over intellect is the story of Gary and Mary Chauncey, a couple whose last thoughts were to save their child. The Chaunceys had a daughter named Andrea who had cerebral palsy. They were aboard an Amtrak train when it crashed into the river. They pushed Andrea through the train's window to be rescued, but the couple died.

Sociobiologists emphasize the importance of emotions over intellect during critical moments. When faced with an emergency, emotions rule the brain to act on what it feels is right. In the story above, the parents' love for their child led to the decision to save their child.

When Passions Overwhelm Reason

In some cases, passions lead to tragedies, especially if fear overcame a person and acted on impulse. One story that demonstrates this is when Bobby Crabtree accidentally shot his daughter when surprised. Bobby and his wife arrived home at one in the morning, and they thought that their daughter Matilda was staying with friends. Fear overcame Bobby when he heard noises in the house, and impulsively shot Matilda in surprise before he could recognize her voice.

This impulsive action stems from our basic survival instincts. Many publications have been written to try to contain emotions and not develop them. Some examples are the Ten Commandments of the Hebrews, the Code of Hammurabi, and the Edicts of Emperor Ashoka. Personal histories and past events affect our rational judgment, which may cause tragedies.

Impulses to Action

There are also instances that fear saves you. One instance is when you are stuck in a snow flurry, and you decide to stop for fear of moving on and encountering more danger.

Some physiological reactions prepare emotional responses. For example:

Anger causes increased blood flow to the hands, the heart rate increases, and hormones cause an adrenalin rush. This results in quick impulses and sudden strength to hit someone or grab a weapon.

Fear increases blood flow to the muscles, which prompt you to run away quickly. It could also cause you to freeze and become more alert.

Happiness inhibits negative emotions and makes it easier to relax and recover quickly. Love generates feelings of arousal, tenderness, and sexual satisfaction. It also results in calmness and contentment that causes cooperation.

Other physical responses such as the raising of the eyebrows when shocked, wrinkling the nose when disgusted, or loss of energy during sadness prepare people for the next steps.

How the Brain Grew

The brain evolved from the primitive brain to the brainstem that houses the emotional centers, to the limbic system that is responsible for memory and learning. In the primitive times, the sense of smell was the most powerful and decided whether there is danger, food, or a sexual mate. The second layer of cells directs the body to respond. Since Homo sapiens has a larger neocortex than other species, this means that there are feelings coupled with thinking. The emotional brain causes relationships to either bond or become awry.

Chapter 2: Anatomy of an Emotional Hijacking

Emotional hijacking happens when the limbic system creates an emergency and leads a person to react impulsively without logic. Such happened when Robles, a recently paroled burglar, decided to break-in inside an apartment due to the need for money. He got scared when the tenant threatened that he would be caught. He killed her along with the other tenant who arrived. Decades after that, Robles shared how he was overcome with panic and could not think.

However, there are also emotional explosions that are positive. One example is when reacts with laughter to a hilarious joke or feelings of extreme happiness and excitement.

The Seat of All Passion

Humans have the amygdala, which in Greek means "almond," which connects to the limbic system. The amygdala is responsible for emotional matters as well as memory and learning. When the amygdala is removed to control seizures, one will become incapable of any emotion and will be unable to recognize emotion. When an animal's amygdala is removed, they will no longer experience fear or rage and won't compete or cooperate. Tears are a response to sadness, which an absent amygdala won't cause.

Joseph LeDoux, a neuroscientist from the Center for Neural Science at the New York University, discovered that the amygdala can take control of actions even when the neocortex is still thinking.

The Neural Tripwire

The amygdala is like a neural tripwire that sends out emergency signals to the body. Once the alarm is set off, responses such as the fight or flight response, are triggered. The amygdala is the emotional tripwire that bypasses the brains rational thinking.

The Emotional Sentinel

LeDoux experimented with rats and subjected them to fear the sound of a tone. He paired the tone with an electrical shock, and the rats soon learned to fear the tone even when they do not feel the electric shock.

He also experimented on oddly shaped images that he flashed at people. The images were flashed rapidly that no one could even remember them. At the end of the experiment, LeDoux proved that the amygdala could bypass rational memories.

Because of the experiment, the participants developed an interest in oddly shaped figures without knowing why.

Research shows that the first few seconds are crucial and can be linked to emotion. This means that our emotions can think on its own and propel us to like or dislike something based on the first few seconds.

The Specialist in Emotional Memory

The hippocampus works with the amygdala in retaining facts when faced with emotional situations. In an emergency, the hippocampus helps you recognize faces and places, and the amygdala lets you know if these are favorable or not.

Out-of-date Neural Alarms

The amygdala is responsible for psychoanalytic thoughts rooted from childhood. At birth, the amygdala is almost fully matured. This explains the emotional outbursts, panic, trauma, or phobias that people experience. This is where the neural alarms need improvement because the amygdala is quick to send out emotional responses without knowing why. Therefore, the greater the arousal to the amygdala, the more that the memory of the situation imprints.

When Emotions are Fast and Sloppy

During emergencies, the neural responses bypass the

neocortex and go from the senses to the thalamus and amygdala. This quick response triggers the body to act even before the neocortex realizes what is happening.

In primitive times, this reaction saved the lives of our ancestors. However, these reactions are all snap reactions and executed without much thought. This is why they are called precognitive emotion. It means that people react right away without making sense of what is happening. It is otherwise known as emotional outbursts.

The Emotional Manager

The prefrontal lobes act as the emotional manager and govern emotional reactions. The prefrontal lobes are responsible for planning and organizing, including emotions. In the past, the prefrontal lobes were surgically removed through lobotomy, as these were believed to cause mental illness. The result was an individual who cannot experience any emotions.

The left prefrontal lobes regulate unpleasant emotions, while the right prefrontal lobes are responsible for the negative emotions. In short, the prefrontal lobes work with the amygdala and dictate how it should react. The connections between the limbic system and prefrontal lobes are crucial in fine-tuning emotions and decision-making.

Harmonizing Emotion and Thought

A neurologist at the University of Iowa College of Medicine, Dr. Antonio Damasio, studied patients whose prefrontal-amygdala circuits were damaged. Based on his studies, they made terrible business and personal decisions, but they still had high IQ. He explains that when the neocortex loses touch with the amygdala, emotional reactions are absent.

On the other hand, when emotions crowd people's judgment, we use the term "we can't think straight." This explains why children who are emotionally distressed may become violent, show poor performance in school, and show anxiety.

Part Two:

The Nature of Emotional Intelligence

Chapter 3: When Smart is Dumb

One of the situations that show the importance of emotional intelligence over IQ is the stabbing incident at a high school in Coral Springs, Florida. A sophomore student named Jason stabbed his physics teacher, David Pologruto, because he received a grade of 80 on a quiz. He believed that a B grade would get in the way of his dreams in going to Harvard medical school. As a result, he went to school with a butcher knife and confronted Pologruto. The judge, a panel of psychologists and psychiatrists, claimed that he was partially psychotic. Jason's accounts were also different from that of Pologruto. Jason said that he was planning to commit suicide. However, Pologruto said that Jason was upset about the grade and planned to kill him.

Jason transferred to a private school and graduated at the top of his class. Jason took advanced courses and increased his GPA to 4.61, which is more than A+. However, he never took responsibility and apologized for his attack on Pologruto.

In the book "The Bell Curve," Richard Herrnstein and Charles Murray, points out that for an individual who has an SAT math score of 500 will only be successful in math if he or she puts his heart into it. Emotional intelligence means that you can motivate yourself and overcome frustrations to achieve your dreams. An emotionally intelligent individual can also regulate his or her emotions, delay gratification, and avoid mood swings that may cloud rational judgment.

Emotional Intelligence and Destiny

Based on statistics, 81 valedictorians and salutatorians from Illinois high schools in 1981 reached average success in their late twenties. High IQ does not prepare the graduates for the turmoil and challenges that life brings.

A Different Kind of Intelligence

At the Elliot-Pearson Preschool inside the campus of Tufts University, experts developed a specialized curriculum that targets all kinds of intelligence. Judy, a four-year-old, was a student of Project Spectrum in this school. The goal was to hone children's abilities beyond the three R's. At an early age, Judy showed social intelligence where she is a keen observer of her classmate's social activities. When they played the Classroom Game, Judy was able to associate which of her classmates played in specific areas of the room and even matched their best friends. The skills that Judy displayed at an early age is a classic example of "people skills" that will enable her success in different fields from sales, to management, to diplomacy.

Project Spectrum was the brainchild of Howard Gardner. Gardner is a psychologist at the Harvard School of Education who believed that children should not be ranked; instead, their natural competencies should be developed into talents.

Furthermore, Gardner was the proponent of the multiple intelligence theory, that there is not just one kind of intelligence, but seven. These kinds of intelligence are based on an individual's abilities, competencies, and interests. Mental intelligence is just a score and that the Stanford-Binet Intelligence Scale is not an accurate predictor of successful performance in various activities.

Gardner further breaks down the multiple intelligences into two categories. First, the "interpersonal intelligence" which is the ability to understand people and work cooperatively with them. This type of intelligence allows people to understand and respond appropriately. Second is the "intrapersonal" intelligence, which is a view of one's self, and how he or she can use that model and function effectively. This means that an individual uses self-knowledge and uses it as a guide for behavior.

Spock vs. Data When Cognition is not Enough

In Star Trek, two characters best explain how important feelings are. Mr. Spock, a hyper-rational being, embodies that

13

emotions mess up intelligence. On the other hand, Data realizes that pure logic is unable to provide the right solution when there are no feelings involved. Furthermore, Data can expertly play music or write poetry but could never feel any passion towards it.

Gardner further states that personal intelligence were more like the emotions. He emphasizes that emotions are crucial in forming relationships and making crucial decisions in life. Therefore, children need to enhance their personal intelligence, too.

Can Emotions be Intelligent?

Peter Salovey, a Yale psychologist, expands Gardner's multiple intelligences into five areas:

1. Self-awareness – The ability to recognize true feelings and make decisions such as choosing a marriage partner or job.

2. Managing emotions – How to react appropriately based on true feelings and not feel distressed.

3. Self-motivation – How to control and motivate oneself based on feelings to become more productive and effective.

4. Recognizing others' emotions – Showing empathy and responding to others.

5. Managing relationships – Being able to manage others' emotions and interact smoothly with others.

IQ and Emotions Intelligence: Pure Types

IQ and emotional intelligence are two separate competencies. The main challenge is that there is no standard pen-and-paper test to measure emotional intelligence accurately. To illustrate, here are the differences between people who have high IQ and high EQ.

People with high IQ is ambitious, productive, and untroubled by his concerns. They are also fluent in expressing their thoughts and value intellectual interests. However, they tend to be emotionally detached, introspective, anxious, and unable to express their anger openly.

People with high EQ are outgoing, not worrisome, cheerful, assertive, express their feelings appropriately, feel good about themselves, and easily communicate with others.

Of the two intelligences, emotional intelligence makes us more human and allows us to relate well with others and feel happier.

Chapter 4: Know Thyself

Psychologists coined two terms that relate to knowing oneself. First is metacognition, which is one's awareness of thoughts. The other is meta mood, which is one's awareness of emotions. These two terms are more aptly known as self-awareness. Freud calls this the "evenly hovering attention" and allows the individual to become aware of his emotions and respond appropriately with words or actions.

Furthermore, self-awareness allows us to operate from a "meta" position. Meaning, we know what is happening and acknowledge it. It is like saying "I am angry now" even as you experience it. For example, when you stop a child from hitting a playmate due to anger, you only stop the action but don't do anything about the anger.

A psychologist from the University of New Hampshire, John Mayer, presented distinctive styles on how people can deal with emotions:

- Self-aware – These people are aware of their moods and emotions, experience clarity of emotions, and have a positive outlook. When they feel bad, they know how to deal with it because they are aware of why they feel that way.

- Engulfed – These people feel overwhelmed and do not know what to do with their emotions.

- Accepting – One classic example is depression. People are aware of their emotions but do nothing to address it. There are also people who may seem to be in a good mood all the time and do not feel a need to change.

The Passionate and the Indifferent

A psychologist at Temple University, Suzanne Miller, developed a test that assesses a person's reaction when subjected to emergencies. She wanted to know if the person would become vigilant, try to distract themselves or tune out the events.

On the other hand, a psychologist at the University of Illinois, Edward Diener, studied the intensity of emotions that people experienced based on the above situations. He observed that there were people without passions and did not experience any urgency during emergencies. Others who felt extreme emotions such as excitement or anxiety that they would act impulsively.

The Man without Feelings

In 1972, Dr. Peter Sifneos, a Harvard psychologist, introduced the term alexithymia, which is an inability to express emotions. An example is Gary, a smart and successful surgeon, who was described as emotionally flat. Another example is a woman who saw a very sad movie but could not comprehend why she was crying.

Dr. Sifneos proposed that alexithymics can show emotion but are unable to determine or make sense of how they feel. They also lack words in expressing emotions. He stated that this could be due to the disconnection between the neocortex and limbic system by way of surgery. He further explained that these people had no fantasies and were disturbed with the bodily sensation brought about by emotions.

In Praise of Gut Feeling

Elliot was once a successful corporate lawyer who had prefrontal surgery due to a tumor on his forehead. After the surgery, he seemed like a different person who exhibited computer-like thinking. Intellectually, he was still the same. However, when he consulted the neurologist Damasio, it appears that the surgery disconnected the communication with the amygdala. Thus, Elliot became impassive and emotionally unaware and could even talk about his tragedies without showing any feelings. As a result, Elliot lacks the emotional awareness or "gut feeling" when making decisions.

Plumbing the Unconscious

Howard Gardner's inspiration for his theories is Sigmund Freud. Freud is the proponent of psychoanalysis and tells us that emotions are rooted in the unconscious mind. Freud pointed out that emotions start in the unconscious mind and have a powerful impact in our consciousness. Therefore, emotional awareness is the fundamental building block of emotional intelligence.

Chapter 5: Passion's Slaves

In the early times, the Greeks and the Romans aimed to restrain emotional excess. They saw the significance of emotions in life; that passions remove the dullness from life. Aristotle observed that the emotions must be controlled because extreme and uncontrolled emotions lead to anxiety, rage, and extreme agitation.

People must also experience difficulties to maintain balance. This is where the difference between emotional and mental intelligence becomes more evident. Intelligence does not affect people's emotional well-being.

People should manage their emotions and manage mood as well. Managing moods and emotions are an integral part of everyday routine. Psychoanalytic thinkers such as D.W. Winnicott and John Bowlby believe that soothing oneself is a skill and can be learned even as infants.

Furthermore, people cannot control what emotions and when emotions will happen. Rather, people can control how long these emotions can last.

The Anatomy of Rage?

Anger is one of the most difficult to control. One of the

characteristics of anger is that it is both exhilarating and energizing. There are also many effects of anger such as outrage or revenge. Also, the more that people brood, the more justifiable reasons they can think of for anger. However, seeing the situation positively helps stop anger. For example, thinking that the other driver who almost collided with your car might have a medical emergency. Benjamin Franklin accurately observes that "Anger is never without reason, but seldom a good one."

A psychologist from the University of Alabama, Dolf Zillman, finds that the need for survival triggers anger. When one is threatened, treated unjustly, or insulted he or she feels endangered, and thus, angered. This feeling elicits the fight or flight response.

Zillman also conducted a study and proved that people who were provoked had a better chance of getting angry when faced with another unpleasant situation. Zillman also states that anger builds up on anger and may cause rage or even violence.

Zillman proposed that there are two ways to diffuse anger. First is to challenge the thoughts that angers the individual. Second, mitigating information should be presented in the early stages, otherwise known as de-escalation.

Another method of addressing anger is cooling down. Physical activities such as exercise and walking not only changes the body physiologically but also provides distractions. Reading and watching TV or movies are also good distractions. The goal is to get away from something or someone that is the cause of anger. The trick is to become self-aware and determine what causes anger. The best way is also to write these thoughts down, so they avoid building up into a rage.

A Tibetan teacher, Chogyam Trungpa, said that the best way to handle anger is not to act on it and not to suppress it. Contrary to what people believe in, catharsis is not a beneficial way to deal with anger because it does not dispel anger but only satisfies it.

Soothing Anxiety: What, Me Worry?

Two psychologists from the Pennsylvania State University, Thomas Borkovec and Lizabeth Roemer, studied worrying. They established that chronic worrying is the root of all anxiety and may cause disorders such as compulsions and obsessions, phobias, and panic attacks.

There are also two forms of anxiety. First is cognitive anxiety where the mind is filled with worrisome thoughts, one manifestation is insomnia. Second, somatic anxiety is the physiological symptoms such as muscle tension, racing heart, and sweating. Chronic worriers have never-ending worries and are a product of one's thoughts.

There are six steps suggested by Borkovec that can help chronic worriers. First is to become aware of their worries and of the physiological reactions they experience. Second, they must practice relaxation techniques whenever they encounter these episodes. Next, one must challenge the worrisome thoughts and be critical. The goal is not to let the worries become repetitive because they become more powerful. On the other hand, medication may be required for those who have developed anxiety disorders.

Managing Melancholy

Sadness, melancholy, or bereavement has its benefits if there is a realization of the sense of loss. It becomes a self-reflective period, and after this, new actions and goals take place.

However, if the sadness or bereavement becomes a depression, the individual cannot function well. The person may experience confusion, self-hatred, anxiety, and memory lapse. The physical effects are insomnia and restlessness. Some people even worry about what depresses them, which adds to the depression.

Men and women differ in handling sadness. Women tend to become depressed, while men become alcoholic. Cognitive therapy is used to treat depression wherein individuals are taught to challenge their ruminations; and second, to come up with pleasant distractions.

People cope with sadness in many ways. The first, which is also a basic response, is crying, also known as "a good cry." Crying decreases the brain chemicals that are responsible for distress, but only breaks the spell of sadness. Crying only prolongs the sadness and the person will remember it after crying.

Aerobic exercise is another coping method for some people. However, this method only works for those who do not exercise regularly. For those who are physically active, the opposite happens. Physically active people tend to become depressed when they miss a day at the gym. Exercise increases the physiological arousal of people.

Other coping methods are listening to music, taking hot baths, eating their favorite food, shopping, or resorting to sexual pleasure. Methods that are more effective are participating in volunteer work and even praying. When people are depressed, they feel uplifted when helping others because of the fulfillment and the realization that they are luckier.

Repressors: Upbeat Denial

The sentence-completion test measures repressions such as aggression. A psychologist named Daniel Weinberger researched on people who elicited a calm demeanor. In his studies, he found out that people tend to tune out negative emotions such as anxiety and anger. It could be a means of survival or learned behavior from parents.

Davidson also conducted a study and presented that the right brain is responsible for processing negative emotion, while the left brain is the speech center. Davidson calls this positive dissociation or upbeat denial of negative emotions as "unflappableness."

Chapter 6: The Master Aptitude

There are instances that fear overwhelms, and instead of overcoming it, people tend to freeze and become mentally incapacitated. Studies show that the students who experience negative emotions such as anger, depression, or anxiety have trouble learning.

On the other hand, some people use positive motivation to overcome the negative feelings. Examples are athletes, musicians, and grand chess masters. These people also trained early in life, which resulted in success.

Culture also plays a role in aptitude and intelligence. In Asia, the culture is that if you get low grades, you must study more at night. If you still don't improve, you must get up early in the morning to study. In American culture, parents are more accepting of their child's weaknesses and work on developing the strengths. When enthusiasm, persistence, and pleasure motivate people, they can overcome anxiety and succeed. Therefore, emotional intelligence greatly affects an individual's capabilities.

Impulse Control: The Marshmallow Test

In 1960, Walter Mischel conducted the famous

"marshmallow test." The goal was to test delay of gratification in four-year-olds and determine how they would fare later in life. Based on the studies, the children who were able to resist the impulse to eat the marshmallow right away did well when they reached high school. Resisting impulses in childhood is a sign of becoming more self-assertive, confident, trustworthy, and dependable. They also showed better-coping methods when it comes to frustrations.

Foul Moods, Fouled Thinking

In the 1960s, Richard Alpert studied test anxiety. He, along with his colleague Ralph Haber, found out that two kinds of anxiety applied to them both. Alpert's test anxiety hampered his cognitive ability due to anxiety. Haber, on the other hand, became motivated to perform well due to anxiety.

Hypomania is a condition that helps people prevent anxiety. A mildly elated state is most beneficial for writers and artists because it helps them become creative and imaginative. If it gets out of control, it becomes euphoric and leads to anxiety.

On the other hand, good moods allow a person to solve a problem creatively. Mood changes, no matter how mild, plus foul mood clouds judgment and may lead to uncontrollable emotions and bad judgment. A person must learn to be optimistic to handle these negative thoughts.

27

Pandora's Box and Pollyanna: The Power of Positive Thinking

When Pandora accidentally released all evils of the world due to curiosity, she left a significant antidote, which is hope. A psychologist from the University of Kansas, C.R. Snyder, studied hope and its correlation with academics. He determined that students with high hopes set better goals and did better. He showed that hope, as a positive attitude, was a better predictor of grades than SAT scores. Hopefulness is a characteristic of emotionally intelligent people because they do not easily give up to negative emotions.

Optimism: The Great Motivator

Studies show that optimists strive to do better even when faced with hurdles or failures. Albert Bandura, a psychologist from Stanford, researched on self-efficacy and concluded that how people view their abilities determine their success.

Flow: The Neurobiology of Excellence?

Mihaly Csikszentmihalyi, a psychologist from the University of Chicago, coined the term "flow." Athletes call this state being "in the zone" wherein they can perform effortlessly and tune out distractions. Experiencing a state of flow is the peak of emotional intelligence. People become self-absorbed in a task or project that they "forget" about everything else even bodily needs. These people are highly focused and very relaxed, which results to a perfect outcome. People who experience the "flow" are skilled in what they do.

Learning and Flow: A New Model for Education

Howard Gardner, the proponent of multiple intelligences, recommended that students should be motivated internally rather than rewarded. He stated that the flow model would allow students to love studying, avoid getting bored, and perform better. Getting in the flow would prevent students from distracting emotions.

Chapter 7: The Roots of Empathy

In one of the previous chapters, you read about Gary, an alexithymic surgeon who lacked empathy. Self-awareness leads to empathy. Empathy allows people to decipher and understand other people's emotions and respond appropriately. Verbal and non-verbal cues are important when showing empathy. Women are better than empathy than men. Empathy is a sign of emotional intelligence.

How Empathy Unfolds

Empathy is already evident during infancy. Infants are sympathetic to emotions around them. Empathy disappears around two years of age due to upbringing. Infants who experienced awareness of how their actions caused distress to others became more empathic. Others' responses to distressing situations also affect feelings of empathy.

The Well-Attuned Child

A psychiatrist at the Cornell University School of Medicine, Daniel Stern, studied the small gestures and repetitive communication between mother and child. In this study, he found out that a mother's attunement also shapes the child's emotional intelligence later in life. Emotional attunement leads to affection and emotional connection.

The Costs of Misattunement

Lack of emotional attunement in a child causes emotional neglect and dulls empathy. Studies of most criminals are proof of the effects of misattunement. Babies learn to mirror moods of people around them, specifically that of the mother.

On the other hand, some people received emotional abuse become hypersensitive to others' emotions and develop a "borderline personality disorder."

The Neurology of Empathy

Most psychologists studied the correlation of the different parts of the brain with empathy. The right frontal lobes were responsible for deciphering emotions in words, such as the difference between a sarcastic "thanks" and an angry "thanks." The left frontal lobe is responsible for conveying feelings. Studies even showed that monkeys can also read emotions based on facial expressions due to the amygdala and its association with the prefrontal lobes.

Empathy and Ethics: The Roots of Altruism

Martin Hoffman researched on empathy and found out that it is the root of morality. Empathy allows people to share others' distress and become motivated to help them. The opposite of empathy is antipathy. There is also such a thing

31

as empathic anger wherein one feels the need to retaliate and achieve justice for wrongdoing. The level of empathy also has something to do with moral principles.

Life without Empathy the Mind of the Molester the Morals of the Sociopath

Criminals such as molesters and rapists do not feel empathy towards their victims. They think that if the victim does not want to engage in the acts, they could have stopped it. They fail to feel from the victims' perspectives. One Vermont prison psychologist, William Pithers, developed a therapy that changes the perspectives of inmates.

On the other hand, psychopaths or sociopaths do not feel any empathy or compassion at all so the above intervention may not work. Most psychopaths do not even feel fear. A psychologist at the University of British Columbia, Robert Hare, discovered that psychopaths have irregularities in the amygdala, which explains the lack of fear and remorse.

Chapter 8: The Social Arts

The basis of emotional intelligence can start at a young age. Take the story of a toddler who resorted to different strategies to calm his older brother. At a young age of two and a half, he is sensitive to others' feelings and does his best to handle somebody else's emotions. This means that the toddler has self-awareness even at a young age. People skills stem from attunement, self-control, and patience, which leads to effective interaction with others.

Show Some Emotion

Emotional displays are based on "display rules." The first one is not showing emotion when an authority figure is present. The second rule is exaggerating what one feels. The third is replacing the feeling with another, such as the inability to say "no." Education, instruction, and culture significantly affect these rules.

Expressiveness and Emotional Contagion

Emotions are contagious and are affected by the degree of emotional rapport. People also imitate others' moods or emotions unconsciously. Dominant people can affect others' moods and emotions by affecting the other person's emotional state through facial expressions, the tone of voice, and actions.

The Rudiments of Social Intelligence

Hatch and Gardner pointed out four abilities that compose interpersonal intelligence:

- Group organization – leadership, involves managing a network of people. An example is a child who takes the lead in decisions of what to play.

- Negotiations that lead to solutions – mediators prevent and resolve conflicts.

- Personal connections – empathic people make good team players and partners. They are adept at recognizing and understanding emotions.

- Social analysis – establishing rapport based on others' feelings, concerns, and motivations.

On the other hand, there are social chameleons who, at face value, seem to possess the above characteristics but resort to doing something else other than what they did. Social chameleons are only concerned with success and they do these by being focused on creating good first impressions.

34

The Making of a Social Incompetent

Children who have dyssema, those who are unable to decipher non-verbal signals, may lead to social deficiencies. The causes may be underlying childhood fears, bullied due to being "strange," or cannot read and understand emotions. These children also function poorly in school due to social isolation.

"We Hate You": At the Threshold

At a young age, children learn to join groups. First, a child may try to join by taking the lead right away. This method does not work with the group especially if the child is a newcomer. Second, he or she may exercise caution and observe the activities before trying to "fit in" by imitating what a group member is doing. The second method shows being sensitive to others, thus establishing acceptance and connection.

Emotional Brilliance: A Case Report

Handling anger and empathizing with him is the peak of emotional brilliance. Such is the story of a man named Terry who studied Aikido lessons in Japan. He was ready to use his skills to calm a drunk but was surprised when a senior man was able to pacify the man. The old man's strategy was to relate to the drunk man and encouraged him to share his feelings. In this way, the old man not only pacified the drunk but determined the cause of his violent behavior.

Part Three:

Emotional Intelligence Applied

Chapter 9: Intimate Enemies

Statistics show that couples who are married in the 90s have a 67% chance of ending up in divorce as compared to those who got married in the 1890s. Not only does the decline of emotional intelligence affect marriage, but also the beliefs about divorce and wives' economic dependence on their spouses.

His Marriage and Hers: Childhood Roots

The emotions of a couple in marriage stem from childhood upbringing and social norms. At a young age, boys and girls do not have specific preferences when it comes to the opposite sex. As they grow older, they fear being teased on having a "boyfriend" or "girlfriend." At the age of seven, boys and girls rarely have friends of the opposite sex. They only mingle again during the dating period.

Parents also speak more openly about emotions to their daughters than their sons. Another factor is that girls' verbal language develops faster than boys do. As a result, girls can better handle their emotions by talking about them and voicing them out. Boys, on the other hand, result in confrontation.

At playtime, the differences between girls and boys are also evident. Girls tend to form small groups and are focused on camaraderie and cooperation. Boys' games are more physical and competitive. Boys are even more concerned with their independence, while girls are more concerned with relationships.

These factors affect a marriage, as women are more emotionally ready when entering a relationship. The role of an emotional manager also falls on women, which may create rifts if not handled properly. The key is to disregard gender differences and work towards agreeing on how to disagree.

Marital Fault Lines

In a marriage, facial expressions, criticism, and contempt affect if the marriage will last. When a spouse shows disgust or contempt through facial expressions, even without saying anything, it affects the other and is a sign of divorce. How the other reacts to disappointing actions also affect them. When a spouse attacks the partner's character instead of the actions, it causes embarrassment and hurt feelings.

The fight-or-flight response is also evident because of angry confrontations. Either one partner fights, and it ensues into an argument, or in most cases, the husband would stonewall the wife and retreat into silence. Stonewalling, when done habitually, ruins a relationship because it prevents ironing out disagreements.

Toxic Thoughts

Toxic thoughts ruin a couple's relationship because they trigger the neural tripwire. Thoughts are not discussed openly and result in negative thoughts such as being bullied by a spouse or feeling like a victim. Toxic thoughts also lead to an emotional hijacking and pessimism that ruins the relationship. These lead to feelings of jealousy, bitterness, and mistrust.

Flooding: The Swamping of a Marriage

Flooding means that one spouse is flooded with emotional distress. When one partner feels overwhelmed, the result may be emotional hijacking. The flooded partner also thinks negatively of his or her partner and ruins the marriage.

Men: The Vulnerable Sex

Men are most likely to result in flooding and stonewalling. When a man is flooded, his adrenalin levels increase and is triggered by the wife's negativity in lower levels. Men also recover longer physiologically. Also, men stonewalling as a defense mechanism against flooding. As a result, the wife criticizes the husband, and he resorts to being more defensive.

His and Hers: Marital Advice

Considering these differences, couples need to change their responses when dealing with negativity. Husbands should be open to the fact that anger is not a personal attack. Men also need to show more empathy and listen, rather than offering a practical solution.

On the other hand, women should learn how to voice out their complaints. Be specific on which action is distressing and avoid attacking the husband's character. A personal attack will lead to the husband's stonewalling, and the negative cycle begins.

The Good Fight

Healthy disagreements are all right for a married couple. One or both should focus on de-escalating the issue, empathizing, listening, and calming yourself or your partner. These are essential in a relationship and show emotional competence. These habits take hard work and persistence and do not happen overnight.

One way of calming down is to learn how to soothe oneself. Cooling down by taking a break from each other for a few minutes will lead to a better discussion.

Another method is detoxifying self-talk wherein a spouse

challenges the negative thoughts as he or she becomes aware of them.

Non-defensive listening and speaking are also practical ways to calm oneself and your partner. Non-defensive listening demonstrates empathy. Non-defensive speaking focuses on complaints about the actions and is not an attack on the character.

The best way to de-escalate a fight is to let your spouse know that you acknowledge their feelings.

Chapter 10: Managing with a Heart

In the workplace, emotional intelligence is equally important. For example, all members of a team should be attuned to others' feelings and call out practices that may turn out negatively. Managers, or bosses, should not be dominant and prone to anger because the members of the team may be afraid to communicate with them. Having emotional intelligence is cost-effective because you retain loyal employees, and everyone works together productively.

Criticism is Job One

As a manager, it is important to give constructive criticism with feedback. Give details that allow your team to make improvements and not to embarrass.

Criticism is not a way to motivate someone to do better, in fact, the result is the opposite. Employees who are criticized and not allowed to improve result to stonewalling. They either leave the company or refuse to work with the colleague who criticized them. Criticism is a personal attack on an employee's character.

A psychoanalyst, Harry Levinson, who became a corporate consultant, advised people on the art of critique:

- Be specific by focusing on an incident that demonstrates the problem that needs to be changed. Specify the things that were done correctly and the things that were done poorly, plus some action items.

- Present a solution and suggest them to the employee. Provide means of how to improve.

- Be personal and give feedback, whether positive or negative, in person. In this way, there is an opportunity for clarification s or questions.

- Be sensitive and empathic. Be aware of how the other person responds to your feedback so you can adjust accordingly.

On the other hand, the person receiving the feedback should not feel that it is a personal attack. He or she should say so and ask for clarifications.

Dealing with Diversity

Diversity and prejudice is still evident. At work, employees who have prejudices are required not to act prejudiced towards clients or customers. No matter how much training or workshops a company provides to its employees, biases will still be present.

Prejudices are formed in childhood and are a result of emotional learning. Although some people say that they don't feel anything against blacks, some of them may unintentionally ignore them or feel uneasy around them. Beliefs can be changed, but the feelings that go with it still stay.

Emotional intelligence in the workplace means no biases, harmonious working relationships, and valuing diversity.

Organization Savvy and the Group IQ

A group can also be more functional due to group intelligence. At present, "knowledge workers" work in teams rather than in partners. This leads to more success and productivity in the workplace. A group may standout even though they have the same skills from the rest, mainly due to how well they cooperate and look for support. A highly intelligent group contributes their talents while becoming sensitive to others and not being too eager or passive. Social skills lead to teamwork, self-motivation, self-management, and time management, which are all proofs of emotional intelligence.

Chapter 11: Mind and Medicine

In medicine, doctors and nurses do their best in treating sickness physically. However, in some cases, the patient's emotional state is ignored which leads to more distress and makes them more ill. Medical personnel should also pay attention the how the patients are handling their conditions emotionally. They should provide not just physical care but concern as well. Studies have also shown that happiness makes people healthier. Emotional intelligence also plays a part in health and well-being.

The Body's Mind: How Emotions Matter for Health

In a laboratory at the School of Medicine and Dentistry at the University of Rochester, psychologist Robert Ader discovered that the immune system could counter-attack against sickness. Therefore, when the immune system confuses the body's cells for viruses, the individual develops autoimmune diseases such as lupus or allergies.

David Felten, Ader's colleague, also discovered that the autonomic nervous system links to the emotions and affect the immune system. The hormones released during stress, such as adrenaline and nor-adrenaline, hamper immunity. Therefore, when an individual constantly deals with stress, their immune resistance decreases.

Toxic Emotions: The Clinical Data

Medical evidence shows that people who are anxious and panicky have elevated blood pressure and tend to bleed more during surgery. Doctors recommend that a patient is calm before surgery to avoid further complications and even death.

Studies also show that emotions such as anxiety, depression, sadness, tension, and pessimism increase the risks of certain diseases such as heart disease, peptic ulcers, asthma, headaches, and arthritis.

Anger is one of the emotions that make people more prone to a heart attack. Angry patients recalled incidents that angered them and showed that the pumping efficiency of the heart decreased by 7% or more. The more an individual gets angry, the more it adds stress to the heart due to high blood pressure and increased heart rate. However, suppressing anger is not recommended because it agitates the body and raises blood pressure.

Extreme anxiety makes people predisposed to infections such as colds, herpes, and the flu. Married couples monitored their fights and disagreements within three months. It was discovered that they came down with an upper respiratory tract infection or cold three days after the disagreement.

Depression also causes cancer patients and dialysis patients to regress in health. Most of them died within a few years when they succumbed to depression. Doctors should address depression especially for life-threatening diseases such as cancer and diabetes. People admitted to the hospital and became depressed stayed eight days longer than those who were not depressed.

The Medical Benefits of Positive Feelings

Optimism makes people recover faster than those who are pessimistic. As discussed in a previous chapter, hope has the power to heal. Close relationships also help foster positive emotions and better health. People who are isolated have higher mortality rates due to alcoholism, smoking, high cholesterol, high blood pressure, and obesity.

Emotional support is also beneficial. One example is when women who have breast cancer attend support groups. Those who attended weekly meetings had a better chance of survival.

Bringing Emotional Intelligence to Medical Care

Emotional intelligence in the medical field is crucial. Patients' unanswered questions and anxieties need to be addressed properly, so they understand what's going on and do not feel more anxious. When these concerns are not addressed, the patients become fearful, uncertain, and depressed.

Most hospitals prepare the patients for surgery or other medical treatments through relaxation techniques, helpful information about the procedure, and the recovery process. Hospitals also encourage family members to stay with the patients and have larger and more comfortable room0s. Physicians and nurses are also encouraged to foster a "relationship-centered care" to help their patients recover.

Toward a Medicine that Cares

Here are steps to help medicine gear towards emotional intelligence in practice:

1. Help people manage their feelings of anxiety, anger, pessimism, depression, and loneliness. Providing coping methods to single, and poor working mothers, senior citizens, and those exposed to an environment with high crime rates will lessen the risk of smoking and other forms of abuse.

2. Patients also need psychological care other than physical care. As stated previously, emotions affect the immune system.

A doctor's compassion leads to a speedy recovery for the patients.

Part Four:

Windows of Opportunity

Chapter 12: The Family Crucible

Emotional schooling starts with the family. How parents manage their children's feelings play a significant role in emotional intelligence. Here are some common parenting styles that you should avoid and their alternatives:

1. Ignoring Feelings – Parents should help the child become emotionally competent and at the same time grow closer to them emotionally.

2. Laissez-faire parenting – Parents, should provide alternatives to the emotional response. They should help the child understand their emotions and not just prevent them.

3. No respect for the child's feelings – Parents should acknowledge their child's feelings and help the child manage their feelings. Harsh punishments and criticisms do no good.

Parents should teach their children how to recognize, manage, and handle their emotions.

Heart Start

Babies form their emotional intelligence based on the family environment. When they receive positive reinforcement, they follow instructions easily. Furthermore, here are the key elements that relate to emotional intelligence and show that the child is ready for schooling:

1. Confidence – When a child has self-control and shows mastery. He or she should also believe in succeeding and that adults provide help when needed.

2. Curiosity – Exploration, and learning are pleasurable and good.

3. Intentionality – The child shows persistence and develops a sense of competence.

4. Self-control – The child can show age-appropriate behavior.

5. Relatedness – Being able to communicate well with others, understand, and be understood.

6. Capacity to Communicate – Having a sense of trust and showing pleasure when communicating with others.

7. Cooperativeness – Balancing one's needs and the group's needs.

Getting the Emotional Basics

A mother's interaction with her baby is one of the

foundations of emotional intelligence. When a mother looks lovingly at her child no matter what time of the day, the child develops a connection and sense of trust.

Studies show that maltreated children also have parents who are inept and immature. These children were inattentive, anxious, aggressive, and withdrawn. The first three or four years are crucial in building emotional intelligence.

How to Raise a Bully

Aggressiveness and violence are handed down from parent to child. They seem inherited but are learned from their parents' ways. These children take these learned behaviors to school and to the outside world.

Abuse the Extinction of Empathy

Abused children tend to mirror the abuse towards other children. In a study of children in daycare, abused children would react negatively to other children who cried. Most would react violently, and others would stiffen as if bracing for an attack.

Chapter 13: Trauma and Emotional Relearning

In a tragedy at the Cleveland Elementary School, a shooter named Patrick Purdy went on a shooting spree, killed five children, wounded more than twenty, and then shot himself. The children developed post-traumatic stress disorder and became hypervigilant. Some even had nightmares and feared certain sounds.

Traumatizing events are implanted in the amygdala that it leaves an emotional wound that is very sensitive to triggers such as natural catastrophes or accidents.

Horror Frozen in Memory

The greater the event imprints on the amygdala, the more susceptible to post-traumatic stress disorder. Helplessness also contributes to PTSD; the feeling that you cannot do anything leaves a feeling of trauma. Most victims of PTSD have abused children and war veterans.

PTSD as a Limbic Disorder

Post-traumatic stress disorder is linked to the limbic system. When stress hormone, CRF, released by the pituitary gland makes an individual ready for fight or flight. Over-secretion of CRF causes hyperarousal that triggers past traumatic events. Therefore, war veterans may become extremely anxious at the sound of thunder or a car backfiring.

People affected with PTSD may also be numbed to pain and pleasure due to an increase in opioids. Neural changes in the brain may have a lasting effect on those affected by PTSD.

Emotional Relearning

PTSD is a form of fear conditioning. Fear conditioning is when someone learns to fear something because it is associated with a negative experience. Extinction of the fear gradually happens when the trigger does not lead to a traumatic experience. The fear itself is still there but is suppressed by the amygdala. Richard Davidson, a psychologist at the University of Wisconsin, discovered that people with high activity in the left prefrontal region could cope better and recover from PTSD.

Re-educating the Emotional Brain

People living with PTSD can recover by reeducating the brain. Adults and children have different approaches when handling stressful events. Adults may tend to block out traumatic memories; children deal with them through play. Replaying the traumatic events through play helps them gain power and overcome the trauma. A child psychiatrist named Spencer Eth, asks his patients to draw any picture. Through drawings, the child can release his thoughts therapeutically.

Emotional Relearning and Recovery from Trauma

There are three steps towards recovery from emotional trauma:

1. Regaining a sense of safety - This equates to finding coping methods and seeking help. Some therapists may offer medication to help them deal with anxiety and sleeplessness.

2. Remembering the traumatic details – This helps the patient regain control over the situations, retell the situation, and relearn an emotional response to it. The patient is also asked to mourn the loss that was brought about by the trauma.

3. Rebuilding a new life - Turning to trusted people and establishing a mutually trusting relationship helps the individual fully recover. He or she will feel safer and will tend to accept the trauma as a learning experience.

Psychotherapy as an Emotional Tutorial

Emotional learning can be learned throughout life. With

psychotherapy, past events that creep into the unconscious can be addressed. Once aware of these past events or emotions, it is possible to relearn emotional responses.

Chapter 14: Temperament is Not Destiny

Jerome Kagan, a developmental psychologist at Harvard University, points out that there are four types of temperament. These are being bold, melancholy, upbeat, or timid. He discovered that children who are fearful and highly sensitive grow into shy and timid adults.

The Neurochemistry of Timidity

Jerome Kagan further explained that timid children were born with neurochemistry that easily arouses the neural circuit in the amygdala. This results in their being fearful and avoids the unfamiliar. Bolder, braver, and outgoing children are born with a nervous system that has a higher threshold for arousal. Panic attacks are also more evident in puberty.

Nothing Bothers Me: The Cheerful Temperament

As mentioned previously, psychologist Richard Davidson said that people who had high activity in the left prefrontal lobes have a cheerful temperament. On the other hand, people who had higher activity in the right prefrontal lobe were more prone to depression. Given these details, emotional lessons during childhood affect a person's temperament later in life. They either contribute to the temperament or change it.

Taming the Over Excitable Amygdala

Based on Kagan's studies, timid children can become more confident. Mothers play a compelling role in taming the overexcited amygdala. Protective mothers tend to deprive the child of learning to overcome their fears. On the other hand, empathic, direct, and those that give firm limits leads to obedience. Parents who allow their naturally born timid children to handle emotions raise emotionally intelligent individuals.

Childhood: A window of Opportunity

Pruning is s system wherein the brain loses the less-used neuronal connections that children are born with. Compared with adults, children have more neurons, which explains why they are like sponges and are sensitive to the environment. Studies also show that behavioral therapy changes brain functions and "cures" obsessive-compulsive behaviors.

Crucial Windows

Human brains take longer to fully mature. Puberty is the peak of pruning. Sensory brain areas mature fully during childhood, the limbic system matures during puberty, but the frontal lobes develop until about 18 years old. Therefore, emotional intelligence is developed later in life. Habits developed in childhood pave the way on how an individual emotionally matures. Parents should still help their children understand and manage emotions even as they are past the adolescent period.

Part Five:

Emotional Literacy

Chapter 15: The Cost of Emotional Illiteracy

Most victims of emotional illiteracy are teenagers and African-Americans. These individuals are unable to control their emotions well, are subjected to bullying, violence, discrimination, and abuse. Nowadays, depression, eating disorders, teenage pregnancy, and early marriage care becoming common due to emotional illiteracy.

An Emotional Malaise

Based on the above data, more children are resorting to sulking or social withdrawals, depression due to feelings of being unloved or unaccepted, inattention or poor concentration due to anxiety, and aggressive behavior due to the environment and upbringing.

Taming Aggression

Not all angry children become bullies. Some withdraw themselves from society. The common factor among angry children is that they see everyone as a threat. These children are emotionally vulnerable and have a low threshold for being upset. Rejection adds to their anger. The result is hostile or difficult behavior.

School for Bullies

Angry adolescents who resort to bullying are subjected to anger-control sessions that teach them to become self-aware and handle their emotions in other appropriate ways. In the program, they discuss situations that anger them or participate in role-plays. Those who went through the program had a better chance of improving.

Preventing Depression

One cause of depression is lack of assertiveness. Relationships with peers and the family are also factors in teen depression. Since adolescents do not know how to express their emotions, parents have difficulty offering emotional support and guidance.

A Cost of Modernity: Rising Rates of Depression

Industrialization and modernization has contributed to depression. The reason is that it is more difficult to reach out to a supportive family due to an increase in divorce rates. More parents are usually not present at home due to separation, career, or even death. Children are unable to self-identify with important people in their lives.

The Course of Depression in the Young

Depression causes children to withdraw socially and do

poorly in school. Prevent childhood depression instead of treating it to address the problem.

Depressionogenic Ways of Thought

Pessimism in childhood also leads to depression. These children already feel helpless and hopeless and do not believe in their abilities anymore. One main cause is rejection by peers and family members. Divorce also makes a child feel unwanted.

Short-Circuiting Depression

Children are encouraged to challenge their difficulties to prevent depression. Children are subjected to classes that teach them that they have control over their emotions. They are also taught how to handle these negative emotions. Children should learn emotional skills as adolescents.

Eating Disorders

Eating disorders such as bulimia and obesity stem from preoccupation with being thin. Young girls grow up in a society where people believe that thin is beautiful. Obese people, on the other hand, result in eating when they feel anxious, upset, or angry. The technique is to identify these feelings and learn appropriate ways of handling these emotions apart from eating or not eating.

Only the Lonely: Dropouts

Rejection is unavoidable, but a student must learn to handle it well. Most children drop out of school due to social rejection. They also fail to give way to people who want to make amends. Socially rejected children miss the opportunity to develop close relationships and emotional growth.

Coaching for Friendship

Coaching is the best way to help socially rejected children. These children were asked to participate in games and were coached on how to make playing games more fun or how to be friendly and nice. They experience happiness and are encouraged to try out their new skills with other children.

Drinking and Drugs: Addiction as Self-Medication

Experimenting with alcohol and drugs may seem an initiation rite for some adolescents. However, some see this as an escape and means of coping with stress and anxiety. Some may result in drugs due to the easy access or glamor thinking associated with it. Those who are biologically predisposed to alcohol and drugs feel "normal" after the first dose. They seem to find emotional relief in these substances.

No More Wars: A Final Common Preventive Pathway

Emotional competence is learned and can still be taught. Information is helpful, but intervention programs are more beneficial. Prevention is the key to end the never-ending cycle of emotional illiteracy. Emotional competence should start in childhood with the family.

Chapter 16: Schooling the Emotions

Self-science is one of the programs that address emotional-literacy. The focus is on the child's emotions, tensions, and traumas. These classes are interventions designed by psychologists to prevent emotional illiteracy among the youth.

Among the lessons in this class is cooperation, responding to criticism and arguments, handling disagreements, and being aware of one's own emotions and others.

Self-science focuses on managing emotions such as being aware of the cause and how to handle it. Students are also taught the importance of empathy, conflict resolution, and negotiations.

There are still skeptics to this approach. However, in a small private school in Nueva, teachers promote emotional competence to their students. Some teachers infiltrate their lessons with lessons on emotional and social skills. How teachers see and manage misbehavior is another strategy that addresses emotional literacy.

Developmental psychologists even developed a "stoplight" poster that helps students control their impulses:

Red light – pause, calm down, think before acting.

Yellow light – state the problem and your feelings. State a positive goal. Come up with many solutions. Think of the consequences.

Green light- Go and execute the best plan.

Another emotional-literacy program is the PATHS curriculum that designs interventions against violence and crime.

Another goal of schools is to become more caring to compensate for those homes who cannot provide care.

Cultivating character through self-discipline and empathy lead to civic and moral values. These are the ultimate manifestations of emotional intelligence.

Conclusion

Emotional intelligence is very different from mental intelligence. When an individual has a high IQ, it doesn't mean that he is emotionally intelligent. In this book, you have learned about how the emotions and autonomic nervous system are closely related. You also learned about the parts of the brain that are responsible for certain emotions and feelings.

Emotional literacy can be learned, and timing is crucial. The prefrontal lobes are responsible for emotional intelligence and this area matures around 16 to 18 years of age. One must learn to be aware of emotions, handle the emotions, and give an appropriate emotional response. One must also be empathic, understand others' emotions, and learn how to deal with them.

A lack of emotional intelligence is also the cause of violence, crime, eating disorders, depression, and some diseases. Also, those in the medical profession should understand that patients not only need physical care but emotional care. Emotions can greatly affect the health of a person due to the stress hormones that are released, as well as blood pressure and heart rate.

Even though certain temperaments are inborn, environment and parental upbringing can mitigate or develop these temperaments. Emotional intelligence can be honed through relearning and changing habits.

Final Thoughts

Hey! Did you enjoy this book? We sincerely hope you thoroughly enjoyed this short read and have gotten immensely valuable insights that will help you in any areas of your life.

Would it be too greedy if we ask for a review from you?

It takes 1 minute to leave 1 review to possibly influence 1 more person's decision to read just 1 book which may change their 1 life. Your 1 minute matters and we value it and thank you so much for giving us your 1 minute. If it sucks, just say it sucks. Period.

FREE BONUS

P.S. Is it okay if we overdeliver?

Here at Abbey Beathan Publishing, we believe in overdelivering way beyond our reader's expectations. Is it okay if we overdeliver?

Here's the deal, we're going to give you an extremely valuable cheatsheet of "Accelerated Learning". We've partnered up with Ikigai Publishing to present to you the exclusive bonus of "Accelerated Learning Cheatsheet"

What's the catch? We need to trust you... You see, we want to overdeliver and in order for us to do that, we've to trust our reader to keep this bonus a secret to themselves. Why? Because we don't want people to be getting our exclusive accelerated learning cheatsheet without even buying our books itself. Unethical, right?

Ok. Are you ready?

Simply Visit this link: http://bit.ly/acceleratedcheatsheet

We hope you'll enjoy our free bonuses as much as we've enjoyed preparing it for you!

Free Bonus #2: Free Book Preview of Summary: Dreams from my Father

The Book at a Glance

Chapter 1 is all about Barack Obama's origins. He was born to a white mother and a black African father. His grandparents were witness to racial discrimination in the past, and their being liberal-minded and how they respected "colored" people led to his parents union. Although Barack's father left them when he was only 2 years old, his mother and grandparents never spoke ill of him. They still remembered and shared their memories of him as a dignified, intelligent, and graceful gentleman.

Chapter 2 talks about how Barack immigrated to Indonesia when his mother married an Indonesian. In the new country, he turned to his stepfather Lolo for guidance and advice. He learned how to survive, and learned life-long values such as honesty, fairness, and being straightforward. He was also exposed to the cruel world of poverty and violence.

Chapter 3 brings him back to America, where he was required to go to school. His mother stayed in Indonesia with Lolo and his new sister, Maya. She would later join him in America. He would also meet his father for the first time since he left. He would live with him for a month and get to know the father that he never knew.

Chapter 4 shares how Barack went through high school and his experiences living with his grandparents. In fact, he had an eye-opening experience when his grandmother was harassed by a black man on the way to work. As a result, he turned to books trying to search for answers to his identity and on the roots of racism.

In chapter 5, Barack, having found his voice, became active in school rallies. During this time, his mother talked him into building a future by starting college. He would turn to one of his gramps' friends, Frank the poet, and would be warned to keep his eyes open. It was a difficult time, and he further experienced an identity crisis.

In chapter 6, Barack takes the opportunity of a transfer program to Columbia University and transfers to Manhattan. He stays with a Pakistani friend who was an illegal immigrant and became serious about his studies. During the summer, when his mother visited him with Maya, his sister, he would learn of the true story behind his parents' separation and would serve as a realization. He would carry his father's memories even after his death and find a new identity for himself in light of his father.

Chapter 7 talks about how Barack was inspired to become an organizer. He was promoted as a financial writer but later resigned his post. At first, his dreams of becoming an organizer slipped away, if not for his half-sister's phone call that gave him a push. He got hired by a Jewish organizer, Marty Kaufman, and set off to Chicago.

Chapter 8 shows Barack's first few days as an organizer in Chicago. He attended the CCRC rally, which composed of people who were laid off from work. The first few days were full of challenges as there was trouble talking to people and coming up with an issue that everyone believed was worth fighting for.

In chapter 10, Barack was almost ready to give up. However, his and his co-organizers realizations motivated him to do better and make a difference. In the end, he was successful in organizing a meeting with the Mayor's Office Employment and Training (MET), and the result was a promise to have a MET intake center within the vicinity in six months' time.

Chapter 10 speaks of winter, which was a time of realization for Barack. From the stories he heard from the organization leaders, he realized that they were fighting for a cause due to their past – just like him. This led him to open up and relate better to others.

Barack finally meets his half-sister from Kenya, named Auma, in chapter 11. During her visit, she told him things about their father, which made him get to know him from another's point of view. It was in this reunion with her sister that he finally felt free from the memories of his father.

Chapter 12 talks about the success Barack was finally making as an organizer. He eventually separated ways with this boss, Marty. They were able to launch the new MET intake center in Roseland, and also get some young parents involved in fighting for health causes.

In chapter 13, Barack employed a recruit named Johnnie, whom he got along well. He also visited his half-brother in Washington, D.C., and learned more from him. However, Roy's attitude towards their father was more of bitterness.

Chapter 14 talks about how Barack decided to pursue law at Harvard and selected Johnnie to replace him as lead organizer. Their current project was to target the public schools with the help of religious congregations. Barack attended his first ever service and was moved to tears with the realization of hope.

Chapter 15 brings Barack to Kenya, where he meets British men on the plane who were to make up for the "lack of trained professionals" in Kenya. He managed to have his luggage accidentally sent to Johannesburg, and was helped by a lovely stewardess who knew his father. He felt a sense of belonging in Kenya, but the locals still saw him as American.

In chapter 16, Barack meets his other relatives and learns of the rift among his two aunts, Zeituni and Sarah, due to his father's inheritance. He also meets with his half-brother, seventeen-year-old Bernard. Later on, he would meet his father's other wife, Ruth, and his stepbrother Mark, who also studies in America.

Chapter 17 is a family reunion, when Roy comes home to Kenya earlier than expected. Barack and Auma had just come back from a safari, and he was enjoying the last few days of his vacation.

Chapter 18 introduces more of Barack's extended family. He met his grandmother, two uncles, and his grandfather's brother. He also noticed that people would always ask him for something when he arrived. His relatives highly regarded him due to his father's stories about him.

In chapter 19, Barack learns more about his grandfather's discipline and how he prospered due to hard work, about his father's diligence to study abroad, and about the events that happened to his father. He finally understood and felt complete.

The epilogue fast-forwards to the future. Barack pursued law and gave back to the community by helping out community organizers and churches. He met his future wife, Michelle, who was immediately loved by his family. They got married despite some deaths in both their families.

Part 1: Origins

Chapter 1

Barack Obama was named after his father, who was an African Kenyan and a member of the Luo tribe. His father was a smart man who won a scholarship in Nairobi and was among the chosen few who attended university in the United States. He was the first African student at the University of Hawaii, where he graduated at the top of his class, and became president of the International Students Association. He also met his future wife in Hawaii. However, he was asked to go back to Africa for his duties. His son, Barack or Barry, was only two years old at that time. Mother and son remained in the United States.

Barack Junior's mother and grandparents talked fondly of his father. His grandparents told him of a story wherein a white man at the bar was being racist and tried to humiliate his father. His father lectured the man. As a result, the man tried to buy his forgiveness. When Barack was 21, his aunt Jane, who had been a stranger until then, called from Nairobi. She announced that his father had died in a car crash.

One of the things that Barack wondered about was why his mother's parents permitted her to marry his father. Barack's mother was white, and his father was African and black. Eventually, he learned that his grandparents were raised in decent and respectable families, so discrimination was not known. His grandparents also

78

told stories about their past, which were filled with romance, drama, and action. In fact, the stories were always interesting. He also learned that his grandparents eloped just before the Pearl Harbor bombing and that his grandfather enlisted in the army.

His grandfather was also the adventurous type who loved to venture on new starts. He was also poetic and a freethinker. This liberal-mindedness paved the way for his father's invitation to dinner. When Barack's mother invited his father for dinner, his grandfather was struck by his resemblance to his favorite singer, Nat King Cole. When dinner ended, his grandparents commented how dignified, intelligent, and graceful he was – and he also loved his British accent.

When the family moved to Texas, they had their experiences with racial discrimination. These incidents explained why his grandparents allowed his white mother to marry a black man. First was when his grandmother, called Toot or Tutu, spoke with a World War II veteran who was black. She addressed him as Mr. Reed and found him to be very dignified. However, she was called out by the secretary that black men should never be addressed as "Mister". She continued calling him Mr. Reed, but the janitor kept his distance.

Another instance was when his mother came home one day from school and befriended a black girl. The other students threw stones at them and called his mother a "nigger lover". The next day, Barack's grandfather took a leave from work, spoke to the principal, and reported the students who had thrown stones. The principal responded that white girls should not play with colored races.

Eventually, Barack's mother and father were married by a justice of the peace in a quiet ceremony; then, they moved to Hawaii. In Hawaii, there were many different cultures such as Japanese, Chinese, and Filipino. Racism was a thing of the past in Hawaii, and here is where the family became comfortable.

However, Barack still wondered why his father left. His mother and grandparents painted a picture of how amazing he was, but he still did not understand. He even found articles about his father and a photograph of him. Barack felt that something was amiss in his childhood and he grew older, not knowing his father.

Read More…

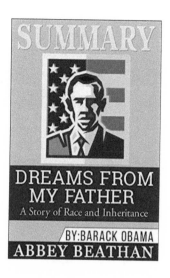